RAISING HALLELUJAH

A **30** DAY DEVOTIONAL
DESIGNED FOR
FAITHFILLED NETWORK MARKETERS

WITH

Jennie Potter

Copyright 2022 © by Jennie Potter
All Rights Reserved

No part of this book may be reproduced or transmitted in any form by any means: graphic, electronic, or mechanical, including photocopying, recording, taping or by any information storage or retrieval system without permission, in writing, from the authors, except for the inclusion of brief quotations in a review, article, book, or academic paper. The authors and publisher of this book and the associated materials have used their best efforts in preparing this material. The authors and publisher make no representations or warranties with respect to accuracy, applicability, fitness or completeness of the contents of this material. They disclaim any warranties expressed or implied, merchantability, or fitness for any particular purpose. The authors and publisher shall in no event be held liable for any loss or other damages, including but not limited to special, incidental, consequential, or other damages.

Individuals making use of this book claim full responsibility for their own personal transformation, health, and well-being as it relates to use of this book. The author and publisher assume no liability and make no promises or guarantees whatsoever for the overall health, well-being, and personal transformation of those making use of this book. If you have any questions or concerns, the advice of a competent professional should be sought.

ISBN: 979-8-9866007-0-3

PRAISE

With faith as her guiding light, Jennie Potter uses her finely-tuned coaching skills to guide and inspire others on their journey to success.

In "Raising Hallelujah," Jennie uses her unique gifts to provide an interactive blueprint for Network Marketers who want to build a thriving business while prioritizing their personal development and spiritual growth.

This book won't just provide the springboard to transform your business, it will transform you - personally, professionally and spiritually.

VANESSA HUNTER | The Brand Muse, Top Consultant for MLM Industry

"Do you feel like you're co-creating a life of success and fulfillment with God? Or do the daily struggles and uncertainty cause you to question whether the Lord is still with you? As a Christian entrepreneur, my life has been filled with fear and uncertainty and often the only thing that got me through was my faith. Yet, we still need inspiration and reminders of who walks beside us at all times. Then, out of nowhere, that prayer was answered by my friend and fellow coach, Jennie Potter. She has created a 30-Day Devotional Plan specifically for Christian network marketers who are passionate about making the world a brighter place. As I began pouring through the inspirational quotes, easy-to-use checklists, and solid coaching advice, I was hooked! I now consider myself a Firekeeper and soon you will too!"

TIM SHURR, MA | Bestselling author of One Belief Away!

Jennie Potter is an amazing coach, speaker and writer, she is passionate about helping others achieve success in their business.

Her step by step "Raising Hallelujah" routine includes prayer, affirmation, praise and taking action.

This devotional is a hands on, deep dive, must read for the Network Marketer who wants to build their business.

RAY HIGDON | Best selling Author of Time, Money, Freedom

Jennie Potter is one of the most positive people I have ever met. In "Raising Hallelujah", she will show you how to turn positivity into positive production by simply keeping your fire burning.

Jennie will show you that through daily affirmations, your belief and fire will never dim if you take daily action.

Looking through Jennie's eyes and perfecting a daily routine, you will become more focused than ever before in reaching your predetermined outcome. "Raising Hallelujah" will help any network marketer navigate the stepping stones necessary for ultimate success.

STEVE SCHULZ | Author of Yes, Sometimes It Is About The Money

TABLE OF *Contents*

GIVING THANKS...5

WHAT IS A FIREKEEPER...........................8

HOW TO USE THIS DEVOTIONAL................10

RAISING HALLELUJAH............................12

    ON *PATH* DAILY...............................13

    FUELING *FIRES* DAILY..............................18

DRY GROUND...24

TWO STICKS..38

THE SPARK..52

FUEL FOR THE FIRE..............................66

INVITING TO THE FIRE.............................80

MANNING YOUR FIRE............................94

RESOURCES...108

GIVING *Thanks*

I am so grateful for the guidance and mentorship both God and the people in my life have given on this journey to help me write this devotional and build a successful business. I am especially grateful to my family—Dave, Hannah, and Kai—who cheer for me always, dream with me, and believe with me. Dave, your unconditional love, cheering, and support have been instrumental in my being able to follow my dreams and live a God-filled, purposeful life. You are my best friend, my person, my love; I consider our love and our family God's greatest gift, and I am so excited for future adventures, new growth, new mountains, new views, and new inspiration.

Not only has God provided many answered prayers along the way, but he has also provided amazing mentorship. I am incredibly grateful to a few people who God placed in my life as answers to prayer, mentors who believed in me before I did, and leaders who encouraged me to be myself.

I am grateful to my mom who has supported and loved me through all the ups and downs. Thank you, Mom. I love you. You have always set an example of how a woman can be a leader, a pilot, and a copilot and wear hiking boots or high heels and do anything she sets her mind to. I am grateful for the unfailing love and support you and Dad provided. I am grateful to you and Michael for setting an example of beautiful love and second starts. I am also incredibly grateful to Irene and Ben Potter who helped me discover who God is and who God can be when you let him in. Your example of faith and love for the Father has made a huge impact on my life.

In business, faith, and friendship I will be forever grateful to Vanessa Hunter whose commitment to seeing other people succeed is a gift. Specific thanks, V, for the hours of mentorship, friendship, meetings, laughter, and growth; you have been my lighthouse, and I will be forever grateful.

FIREKEEPERS with JENNIE POTTER

Steve Schulz, thank you for the gift of belief and accountability from day one; I value our friendship and will always be grateful for your mentorship in building a solid foundation. Thank you for opening doors for me and setting the stage for what is to come.

To my mentor, Ray Higdon, thank you for the example you set when it comes to being vulnerable and hungry for growth. You never stop being coached yourself. You are always searching for new levels and dreaming bigger, always looking for ways to impact the impactors and help more people. I am incredibly grateful to you and your amazing wife. Jessica, you not only lead with a heart for the people but do so with transparency. The desire and action you take to help the children of the world are ever inspiring. I am so grateful for all you have given; you have both changed my life.

There are so many people who have helped in the writing of this, people who have taught me to pray out loud, believe in myself, understand the power of words, brand myself, get into action, embrace God's plan, have patience, deepen my faith and strengthen my courage: Toby and Shelley Bridgman, Kim Guynn, Cheryl Maclean, Candy Gage, Barb Bayne, John Polkowski (in memory), Tara Chapman, Ellyn Klug, Chris Clark (in memory),Craig and Kathy Nelson, Anneliese Dusseldorp, Ronanda Liberty, Paul and Suzie Russo, Sara and Mike Vigil, Melissa Barlock, Phebe trotman, Casey Eberhart, Jules Price, Bill Andreoli, Todd Smith, Andre Vaughn, Renee Brown, Claudette Keller, Joe Kenemore, Blake Graham, Tina Torres, John Maxwell, and Jordan Adler.

To my fellow coaching and speaking team—Andy Louder, Aubrey Cavanaugh, Kaylee Fisher, Jennifer Rajala, Jenny Henrickson, Nicole Domuret, Michelle Mackenzie, Forrest Knight, Mary Kate O'Connell, Mariela Quintanilla, Ryan Brimmer, Staci Hall, and Michelle Eldridge—thank you for your courage to show up daily for the good of all. You continue to inspire, grow, heal, and change lives and have forever changed me.

To all of my coaching clients and team thank you for all the love, support, lessons and for running with me, believing with me and dreaming big alongside of me.

GIVING THANKS

To Margaret Cogswell for the beautiful design of this devotional; you somehow connected with the creative vision in my mind of which I was unable to put into words but you were able to vision for me.

In memory of my father, the mighty oak, who cherished the rain with me, cheered louder than any other, and who I still hear in my heart encouraging me from heaven—I miss your morning calls and feel your pride. This little acorn is becoming the oak, Dad.

WHAT IS A *Firekeeper?*

Years ago, before there were matches, flints, lighters, barbecues, and gas stoves to start a fire, there was only lightning and chance . . . If your tribe had fire, it had to be tended to. Your livelihood, warmth, community, food, and survival depended on it. In those days, there were FIREKEEPERS. The Firekeeper's only job was to keep that fire burning—no matter the rain, the storm, the wind, the wet, or the lack of fuel. Keep that fire burning. Man that fire no matter what.

To be a Firekeeper is to be a Faith-filled Network Marketer, building your business alongside of God. Firekeepers not only do the daily action required to build a successful network marketing business but also lean into the Word and partner with God in all things connected.

I AM FIREKEEPER was born out of a desire to connect with other believers in God who want to succeed in network marketing. Together we will dive into what God says about business, money, courage, consistency, and doing the work alongside him.

God put it on my heart to create a devotional that supports that purpose. Here you will find prayers for your life, your business, and your teams. Here you will find reflection, divine action steps, targeted scripture, prayer, daily practice in Raising Hallelujah, and God-sent inspiration to help you take your business and relationship with God to the next level.

Here we will seek God first and man our fires together. We will start fires, fuel fires, go where the fuel is, and go where the fires are burning. Lean into God, and with his help and two sticks—no matter the rain, the storm, the wind, the wet, or the lack of fuel—keep the fire burning.

WHAT IS A FIREKEEPER

BE A FIREKEEPER AND RAISE HALLELUJAH
WITH ME DAILY.

THEY WILL KNOW US BY OUR FAITH.

THEY WILL KNOW US AS WE
SEEK HIM FIRST.

THEY WILL KNOW US BY OUR
GRATITUDE AND PRAISE.

THEY WILL KNOW US BY OUR INVITATION.

THEY WILL KNOW AND FEEL
US BY OUR WARMTH.

THEY WILL KNOW AND
SEE US BY OUR LIGHT.

FINALLY, THEY WILL KNOW AND
HEAR US BY OUR ROAR.

HOW TO USE THIS *Devotional*

Do not be anxious or worried about anything, but in everything by prayer and petition with thanksgiving, continue to make your requests known to God.
PHILIPPIANS 4:6

Before I was a believer, I found affirmations and would repeat them in the mirror to myself daily. At that time, I was totally lost, totally broken . . . I was so far from loving myself that I was attracting some yucky stuff. My self-loathing and lack of self-respect were mirrored everywhere in my life. As I affirmed my words of self-love, I started to shift. Then I added gratitude daily, and a little over a decade later, I was shouting praise to the Lord, praying out loud, and affirming my "I AM" statements and gratitude at the top of my lungs in the mirror (I was THAT girl) . . . When I became a believer, things really started happening. As my thoughts shifted, my prayers shifted, and things began to manifest at a rapid pace. God answered my prayers: a loving husband, a beautiful family, a business I could do from home, mentors, friends, new team leaders, awards, rank advancements, helicopter rides, opportunities on stage, dream jobs, dream vacations, and dream vehicles, but also, and more importantly, I grew much closer to God and learned about who HE says I AM in scripture. This morning routine became lovingly known as **Raising Hallelujah**, and I would joke that I had found the keys to the kingdom . . . I believe there is some truth in this.

For the next 30 days, create a new habit with me and Raise Hallelujah daily. Do it with joy, do it with excitement, and do it with faith that moves mountains. I have included a prayer, and I encourage you to either pray this prayer each day or make your own version. This is about intentionally asking God for help with building your business, your purpose, and your faith daily.

Each day, write and speak out your **PATH** (PRAYER, AFFIRMATIONS, THANKS, HALLELUJAH) and **FIRES** (FOLLOW UP, INVITE, RECONNECT, EXPAND, SOCIAL

HOW TO USE THIS DEVOTIONAL

POSTS), spend time with the scripture, reflect, and do the divine action step. The core skills you will use daily—no matter your product, opportunity, or service—will be following up with those you have reached out to before, inviting people to take a look at your product/opportunity, reconnecting with warm connections, intentionally expanding your network, and posting on social media.

As this devotional's focus is to strengthen your connection to God in your business, I have added a place for you to mark complete the core action steps daily—your **PATH FIRES** you will want to do alongside your daily scripture/devotion reading. You will find additional suggestions in the resources section for tangible tools for building a successful network marketing business.

DIVINE TIP!

If you are short on time, use a timer for your business tasks! 13 – 15 mins is the ideal amount of time for an average adult to focus on one task. Do your tasks in 15-minute segments for increased productivity and focus. Check out my favorite suggestions in my resource section and subscribe to my blog for tangible ways to invite people to look at your product or opportunity without feeling sales-y, follow up with people without feeling pushy. Explore ways to expand your network and post on social media in a way that feels authentic, creates curiosity, and is in line with who you are.

Your word is a lamp for my feet, a light on my path.
PHILIPPIANS 4:6

RAISING *Hallelujah*

For the next 30 days, Raise Hallelujah with PATH, read and reflect on the devotion, do the divine action step, and keep your FIRES burning daily.

Doing *PATH FIRES daily*

PRAYER

AFFIRMATIONS

THANKS

HALLELUJAH/PRAISE

FOLLOW UP

INVITATION

RECONNECTING WITH

EXPANDING NETWORK

SOCIAL POSTING

PATH FIRES

Prayer for my network marketing business

(use this or create your own)

Lord, I am so grateful for the opportunity to partner with YOU in business. I thank you for guiding me and blessing me with creativity and drive to build this business in a way that honors you. I thank you for helping me do the daily action steps, which bring new customers and partners into this business. I am grateful for the new leaders and customers I am attracting. I ask for your help in connecting me with other like-minded leaders, for leaders who bring new gifts and creativity, for those in need of an opportunity, for those who need our product for a life-changing experience, and for those who need to grow closer to you. I thank you for helping me be coachable, helping me hear your Word, your guidance. I thank you for bringing the right mentorship into my life. I thank you for your favor with my team, my company, my rank, my earnings, my reach. I know if I build this with you that my relationship deepens with you; I thank you for that relationship. I thank you for blessing me with an abundant mindset, open to learning, to growth, and to your love and kindness. I thank you, God, for blessing my team—the team that I will have in the future, the team that I have now, and team members who are no longer active. Favor them, bless them, help them be courageous wherever they are on their paths. Bless the corporate office and all the support staff. Bless them with favor, abundance, and great ideas. I thank you, Lord, for helping me with my focus. I praise you for standing alongside me as I step into my God-given gifts and ask you to help me seek you first.

Today and each day, I stand on the scripture of your Word. Adapted from Philippians 4:8: I will keep my thoughts continually fixed on all that is authentic and real, honorable and admirable, beautiful and respectful, pure and holy, merciful and kind. I will put into practice what I heard and saw and realized through you. And God you who makes everything work together, will help everything work for good in a most beautiful harmony.**

Amen

> **DIVINE TIP!**
> *You can find this .pdf and print out this prayer at*
> *www.iamfirekeeper.com/devotional*

PATH FIRES
Affirmations/I AM statements
What God says about you

Some examples of I AM statements

I am favored by God, I am fully using my God-given gifts, I am attracting leaders and customers to my business, I am abundant, I am a daughter/son of the most high God.

I struggled when I first attempted I AM statements; I could barely look myself in the eye those first days. I had three, and I did not believe them at all: I am beautiful, I am worthy of love, I love myself. I chose those three because, at the time, I had extremely negative thoughts about who I was. Slowly my self-image began to change, and then everything shifted. As things shifted, I added more: I am a speaker, a top leader, I am inspiring millions . . . If you, like me, struggle with this, ask God for help. You are thanking him and praising him for what already is. This is faith. The chapter is already written; go ahead and thank him for the good stuff. Thank him for vacations, leaders, and inspiration; thank him for projects and upline and downline. Thank him for the future chapters and the current chapter, and thank him for all that brought you here.

One thing that really helped me move into a new appreciation of who I AM and what I am capable of, something that helped me connect with my purpose, was learning what God says about me—what God says about all of us. Throughout this devotional you will find statements pulled from scripture which are examples of who God says you are, write them out, speak them out see yourself as God sees you.

You are . . . straight from the Bible

There is a point in the bible when Moses sends men out to the land which God had promised them to scout it out. the good news? It was an awesome land, a land that flowed with milk and honey... the bad news? There were Giants...

Caleb (one of the scouts) a man of great faith, saw the obstacles and knew they could overcome them with God at their side. "Let's go up and take the land—now. We can do it," but the others said, "We can't attack those people; they're way stronger than we are" (Number 13, MSG).

Specifically, they said, "Alongside them we felt like grasshoppers. And they looked down on us as if we were grasshoppers" (Numbers 13, MSG).

When obstacles stand in your way, are you like Caleb, ready to overcome anything? Or are you like the other men who went to spy out the land, perceiving themselves as grasshoppers and the obstacles as giants. Too often, we see our obstacles as giants and ourselves as mere grasshoppers, helpless to do anything. We will encounter many obstacles as we build our network marketing businesses: people's opinions, fears around selling, fears around shining, succeeding, failing, and many others . . . some real and some just wounded perception.

Do you see yourself as God sees you? Throughout this devotional, I will include days to reflect on straight from the Bible on who God says you are.

In these sections, use the blank beside each statement to write out an I AM statement.

For example:

You are favored by God, **2 CORINTHIANS 6:2**

I am Favored by God

You are a new creation **2 CORINTHIANS 5:17 ESV**

You are a treasured possession **DEUTERONOMY 7:6 ESV**

DIVINE TIP!

Throughout the next 30 days, underline, highlight, or put a star beside the statements you feel will most impact your perception of who you are and, therefore, your life. Where have you been acting as a grasshopper when, in truth, you are a giant? Saying I AM statements in the present tense will help you stand on what God says about you and who you truly are (you will use these and ones of your own creation in your 30 days of Raising Hallelujah),

PATH FIRES
*Giving **T**hanks*

Give gratitude daily for all that you have and all that is coming.

What can you be grateful for that is right in front of your eyes? Start there, then shift to what God has put on your heart. Thank him with the belief that it is already there, that it has already happened. Give gratitude for the future chapters as if they have already happened. It is already written.

Let your roots grow down into him, and let your lives be built on him. Then your faith will grow strong in the truth you were taught, and you will overflow with thankfulness.
COL 2:7 NLT

PATH FIRES
*Raising **H**allelujah/Praise*

hal·le·lu·jah | \ ha-lə-lü-yə \

Definition of *hallelujah* (Entry 1 of 2)
—used to express praise, joy, or thanks, **hallelujah**
noun

Definition of *hallelujah* (Entry 2 of 2)
: a shout or song of praise or thanksgiving

Raising Hallelujah means praising God for what you can see, all that your life has brought you, and all that God is bringing you. Praise God for what you can see with your physical eyes and what you can see as a believer in what is to come.

But as for us, we will bless and affectionately and gratefully praise the LORD From this time forth and forever. Praise the LORD! (Hallelujah!)
PSALM 115:18 AMP

DIVINE TIP!

I love listening to worship music as I do this daily; you can add your favorite.

Call to me and I will answer you, and I will tell you great and hidden things that you have not known.
JEREMIAH 33:3 ESV

PATH FIRES
Following Up daily

Following up with people is a natural next step after we have invited someone to take a look at a video, hop on a webinar, join our FB party, etc. People will often say yes to one of the above invitations and then disappear. It is our job to consistently reach out to people, inviting them to join our opportunity or try our products and then apply a system to stay in touch. It is powerful to have a list as you invite and a system in place to follow up with the people you have invited. I like to use the following system with my follow up: 333—3 days, 3 weeks, 3 months. Reach out 3 days later, 3 weeks later, and then 3 months later. I just put the date I need to follow up with them beside their name. I also geek out with highlighters; feel free to do the same.

See the resource section in this book or go to other recommended tools at iamfirekeeper.com/blog

FIREKEEPERS with JENNIE POTTER

PATH FIRES
Inviting daily

Inviting people to look at our product or opportunity is an important action step required to build a successful business. Having a method and sticking to it daily is powerful. Make sure you have a script that is in your words and a list that you can add to and refer to.

Scripts can help you powerfully build your business if they are designed correctly. It is important to decrease resistance and specifically ask people if they are open or curious to see what we are doing (opportunity or product).

* See the resource section in this book or go to other recommended tools at iamfirekeeper.com/blog

GENERIC WARM MESSAGING: PRODUCT/SERVICE LEAD

Hey, [Name]! I hope you are well; I know it has been forever! I am reaching out to you for a reason. Recently, I found a product/service that has changed my life, and I have been sharing it with others. [INSERT YOUR PERSONAL BENEFIT] (EXAMPLE: I am down 10 pounds, and I've gained back my energy). It's simple to take/apply/use, and I'm loving it. Anyways, I don't know if you would like it, but I'm just curious if you would be open to checking it out? I could fire off a quick video that explains or we could hop on a zoom/call? If you are open, great! If not, no big deal. I hope you are well; stay blessed, and I look forward to catching up regardless!

GENERIC WARM MESSAGING: OPPORTUNITY LEAD

Hey, [Name]! I hope you are well; I know it has been forever! I am reaching out to you for a reason. I found a product/service that has changed my life forever, and I have been sharing it with others. In doing so, I have created a job where I can work from home and show others how to do the same. Anyways, I don't know if you are interested in working from home or earning an additional income, but I'm curious if you would be open to checking it out? If so, I could fire off a quick video that explains what I do, or we could hop on a zoom/call? If you are open, great! If not, no big deal. I hope you are well; stay blessed, and I look forward to catching up regardless!

Both scripts above were adapted from Ray and Jessica Higdon's Social Media Script book.

See the resource section in this book or go to other recommended tools at iamfirekeeper.com/blog

May the LORD bless you and keep you; may the LORD cause His face to shine upon you and be gracious to you;
NUM 6:24, 25 BSB

DIVINE TIP!

Please make these scripts your own authentic voice. They are well designed templates to reduce resistance, but it is still you that is making the invitation. Make sure it sounds like you.

PATH FIRES
*R*econnecting daily

Staying in touch with people in your life helps you strengthen connections, build stronger relationships within your network, and get to know people better and serve where you can, seeing if they need prayer and how they are doing. Reconnecting with past business builders and customers can also be very impactful. Reconnecting with intention is about taking a few minutes or more each day to pour love onto people and let them know you are there for them without any expectation in return.

I like to pray first for God to put someone on my heart who needs to hear from me. Then I go through my list of friends on one of my social media platforms, spend time with my current and past customer lists and current and past business builders.

As this list may feel daunting, I like to set a timer for 15 minutes or more per day, choose one list, and work my way through it. This is about loving on people and being curious, caring, interested.

PATH FIRES
Expanding your Network daily

Each day, go about activities that will bring more people into your network. This does NOT mean sending out friend requests without thought or intention. This IS about following people and connecting with people who are a good fit for your niche, meaning you would love to work with them and they may need your service or product. This IS about joining a few groups and adding value, commenting on posts, and authentically connecting with new people. This IS about attending networking events/groups/communities either online and/or in person and pouring into them.

DIVINE TIP!

Pick 2 or 3 groups/ways to connect with new people for your next 30 days.

PATH FIRES
Social Posting daily

This includes posting or going live on your social media platform of choice once a day and posting on your stories daily to highlight what you are up to (lifestyle, curiosity, value adds), increase exposure, boost your algorithms, and help the people who check you out get a sense of who you are and what you are doing. Stay positive, create curiosity, be authentic, and add value. What posts are you most drawn to? Notice what people like and don't like. Make sure you are in control of what shows up on your news feed. Set your privacy so you can choose if a post goes on your wall or not. I highly recommend NOT selling or posting flyers on your newsfeed; keep selling or posting flyers/invites to your stories and use the 90/10 rule. Ninety percent of your posts should be lifestyle, fun, what you are up to, shout-outs, and curiosity, keeping ten percent of your posts to sales. I would rarely shout out the company name or product name because I want to create curiosity. You want people to reach out to you and ask for more info, NOT to google your products and find them elsewhere. This is not because you are not proud of your company; it is because there are many doors to the same house. About 2 percent will come into your business through the door of an obvious sale or FLYER. About 98 percent will come in because of a story you shared, the curiosity you created, or value you added, etc.

I strongly recommend choosing one social media platform to commit to that you are fueling FIRES with on a daily basis. As a bonus, you can add in other platforms as time allows, but commit to ONE in which you will do the above each day.

Carry one another's burdens and in this way you will fulfill the requirements of the law of Christ [that is, the law of Christian love].
GAL 6:2 AMP

> **DIVINE TIP!**
>
> *Do this devotional with one or more team members, crossline, upline or with other network marketers! start a 30 day group and reflect daily or weekly as you go!*

Again, I give you an eternal truth: If two of you agree to ask God for something in a symphony of prayer, my heavenly Father will do it for you. For wherever two or three come together in honor of my name, I am right there with them.

MATTHEW 18: 19, 20
THE PASSION TRANSLATION

DRY
Ground

WHAT GOD SAYS ABOUT YOU . . .

YOU ARE A TREASURED POSSESSION
DEUTERONOMY 7:6 ESV

I am _____

YOU ARE CHOSEN BY GOD *1 PETER 2:9 NIV*

I am _____

YOU ARE ALIVE TO GOD *ROMANS 6:11 NIV*

I am _____

YOU ARE ANOINTED *1 JOHN 2:27 NIV*

I am _____

YOU ARE THE RECEIVER OF GRACE
JOHN 1:16 ESV

I am _____

YOU ARE BAPTIZED INTO ONE SPIRIT, ONE
BODY *1 CORINTHIANS 12:13 AMP*

I am _____

YOU ARE BEING PERFECTED
HEBREWS 10:14 NIV

I am _____

YOU ARE BLAMELESS *PHILIPPIANS 2:15 NIV*

I am _____

YOU ARE BLESSED *NUMBERS 6:24 NIV*

I am _____

YOU ARE BLESSED WITH ALL SPIRITUAL
BLESSINGS *EPHESIANS 1:3 ESV*

I am _____

God has called you to build your business on a solid foundation.

When we build a fire, we do not build it in a marsh. We find dry ground so that it may stay lit.

Do you know about Nehemiah? His story is epic and inspiring. God called him to do the impossible, to rebuild a giant wall around Jerusalem. It must have seemed an unfeasible task. When he heard the call, he did a few things that helped him succeed.

When Nehemiah (cupbearer to a king of a country far from Jerusalem) heard the conditions of his beloved city and surrounding wall, he was devastated. The first thing he did was fast and pray. Just his prayer alone speaks volumes. He praised God, gave gratitude, asked for forgiveness, then asked for help and favor. He came to the king he served with a request and a plan (he had to travel through enemy lands to get to his city to even start the rebuild). He requested from the king a letter that would give him safe passage, tools, supplies for the journey, and supplies for the rebuilding, all of which the king granted.

When he got to Jerusalem, Nehemiah was met with opposition; people did not think it was possible. He was mocked, yet still, he persisted.

In the rebuilding, he was careful not to listen to the naysayers (the trolls); he planned for success by giving his team a simple blueprint and a daily method of operation. Sure enough, the impossible became possible; brick by brick, they rebuilt the wall.

He heeded the call, he prayed, he asked for support, and enjoyed God's favor. He surrounded himself with positive people who believed in the task at hand, and he refused to listen to the people who wanted him to fail. He gave his team simple tasks, and he consistently showed up day after day and did the work, setting an example for his team. He achieved "the impossible" in just 52 short days with God's guidance and favor.

As you work on your business, you may have already experienced the naysayers; you may be mocked, and there may be opposition to your personal growth, your journey, your goals, and your dreams. Sometimes the bricks can feel pretty heavy and the task at hand unfeasible. But you have God. You, like Nehemiah, have been called to this purpose—to build your business one brick at a time, to find a team to build with you, to follow and give simple leadership and create a simple daily method of operation (DMO). You have favor, and where ever you are in your business, should you include God in the making, you will exceed the improbable.

Starting on dry ground is the foundation with Jesus as the cornerstone and you as the follower, the leader, the favored, the valued, the loved, the redeemed.

I know what it means to lack, and I know what it means to experience overwhelming abundance. For I'm trained in the secret of overcoming all things, whether in fullness or in hunger. And I find that the strength of Christ's explosive power infuses me to conquer every difficulty.
PHILIPPIANS 4:12-13 TPT

DATE _____

Blessed [with spiritual security] is the man who believes and trusts in and relies on the Lord And whose hope and confident expectation is the Lord. For he will be [nourished] like a tree planted by the waters, That spreads out its roots by the river; And will not fear the heat when it comes; But its leaves will be green and moist. And it will not be anxious and concerned in a year of drought Nor stop bearing fruit.
JEREMIAH 17:7-8 AMP

Start from wherever you are and with whatever you've got..
JIM ROHN

Partnering with God in your business and life is the most powerful thing you can do to exponentially increase your growth and realize your potential. Like the root tapped into the stream, when you tap into God, love, inspiration, wisdom, favor, and hope never run dry. YOU have a VIP, all-access pass to the endless source.

REFLECTION: Have I truly asked for God's help in building my business? Do I ask him to bring me leaders, customers, creativity for social media, mentors, guidance? What can I ask of him right now for help specific to my business?

DIVINE STEP FOR SUCCESS

Figure out how much time you need to do the daily activity in your business and then schedule the upcoming week. Where will you fit in your PATH each day? Where will you fit in your FIRES? If your schedule is predictable and you already have a planner, then go ahead and plan the next 4 weeks, where/when will you do your daily activities?

DIVINE TIP!

Check out the resource section for my favorite planner and other tools, go to iamfirekeeper.com

RAISING *Hallelujah*

PATH

- [ ] **PRAY**
- [ ] **THANKS**
- [ ] **AFFIRMATIONS**
- [ ] **HALLELUJAH**

FIRES

- [ ] **FOLLOW UP**
- [ ] **INVITE**
- [ ] **RECONNECT**
- [ ] **EXPAND**
- [ ] **SOCIAL POSTS**

DATE _____

Trust God from the bottom of your heart; don't try and figure out everything on your own. Listen for God's voice in everything you do, everywhere you go; He's the one who will keep you on track. **PROVERBS 3:5-6 MSG**

Faith is to believe what you do not see: the reward of this faith is to see what you believe. **ST. AUGUSTINE**

God has put it on your heart to build a network marketing business and serve the world, yourself, and your family, friends, and connections in this way. When my friend first told me about her opportunity, I was just about to say, "No thank you," when she said, "Jennie, we are changing lives one day at a time," and I felt God tell me to pay attention. Trust that God has put you in the perfect place and has brought you to this moment right now, where you get to hit the reset button if you need to and step into faith and action. What is he calling you to do? You don't have to know the how. You don't even have to know the why. Just lean into that calling. What drew you to this business?

REFLECTION: What drew me to this business? Free write (write whatever comes to mind) what God has put on your heart.

DIVINE STEP FOR SUCCESS

Are you clear on the story you share with others when you present your business and product/service? Sharing your story and knowing other short testimonials is one of the most impactful ways to share. Write out your story. Can you tell it comfortably in under 3 minutes? Does it speak of before (where were you, your pain points), now (what are your results so far), and future (where are you going/goals)? Practice your story in the mirror or on ZOOM; practice key points until you can tell your story comfortably, no matter the scenario.

RAISING *Hallelujah*

PATH

- [ ] **PRAY**
- [ ] **THANKS**
- [ ] **AFFIRMATIONS**
- [ ] **HALLELUJAH**

FIRES

- [ ] **FOLLOW UP**
- [ ] **INVITE**
- [ ] **RECONNECT**
- [ ] **EXPAND**
- [ ] **SOCIAL POSTS**

DATE _____

It takes wisdom to build a house, and understanding to set it on a firm foundation.
PROVERBS 24:3 MSG

You don't have to be great at something to start, but you have to start to be great at something. **ZIG ZIGLAR**

Just as it would be difficult to start a fire in a marsh, it's difficult to do anything without a proper foundation. God's Word is the cornerstone of life. Make this part of your daily mode of operation, leaning into the Word and building your business on a firm foundation. As you set a foundation for your business, ask yourself, "Am I setting a firm foundation for others to get started in their businesses? Do I have a simple process for getting someone started right?

REFLECTION: What do I see as foundational scripture I can lean on for my business? Choose a scripture you can lean on that represents what you need most. Is it courage? Faith? Positive thoughts? There's a scripture for that! What is important to you as you build your business? Foundational? Write out your scripture and why its foundational for you.

DIVINE STEP FOR SUCCESS

What are the steps you have in place to help a new customer or business partner get started? Reflect on how you got started. Write out simply how you get a new customer started. How do you get a business-builder started? Is there a checklist? A short video? Be clear on this process moving forward.

R A I S I N G *Hallelujah*

PATH

- ☐ **PRAY**
- ☐ **THANKS**
- ☐ **AFFIRMATIONS**
- ☐ **HALLELUJAH**

FIRES

- ☐ **FOLLOW UP**
- ☐ **INVITE**
- ☐ **RECONNECT**
- ☐ **EXPAND**
- ☐ **SOCIAL POSTS**

DATE _____

If you're a hard worker and do a good job, you deserve your pay; we don't call your wages a gift. But if you see that the job is too big for you, that It is something only God can do, and you trust him to do it – you could never do it for yourself no matter how hard and long you worked – well, that trusting him-to-do-it is what gets you set right with God, by God. **Sheer gift.** *David confirms this way of looking at it, saying that the one who trusts God to do the putting-everything-right without insisting on having a say in it is one fortunate man.*
ROMANS 4:4-6 MSG

The journey of a thousand miles begins with a single step. **LAO TZU**

Do you get this? Leave the hard work to God. Give Him your worries. Not sure how to reach out to people? Ask him for a mentor. Scared to go live on social media? Ask Him for courage. Don't have a system for follow-up? Ask Him for help. Give it ALL to Him. All of it.

REFLECTION: What am I trying to do on my own that I could use help with? What could I give to God?

DIVINE STEP FOR SUCCESS

Take a moment to ask for specific help in one area in which you feel blocked or feel you "should" not be struggling. Give it to God. Then take that step. Break it into tiny pieces. For example: Not inviting people to check out your opportunity/product? 1. Find a person 2. Click on messenger 3. Paste script to message 4. Hit send. Whatever you are resisting, ask God for help, break it into steps, and do each step one at a time.

RAISING *Hallelujah*

PATH

- ☐ **P**RAY
- ☐ **T**HANKS
- ☐ **A**FFIRMATIONS
- ☐ **H**ALLELUJAH

FIRES

- ☐ **F**OLLOW UP
- ☐ **I**NVITE
- ☐ **R**ECONNECT
- ☐ **E**XPAND
- ☐ **S**OCIAL POSTS

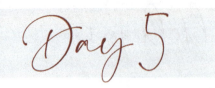

DATE _____

They are not of the world, just as I [John] am not of the world.
JOHN 17:16 AMP

It's not about pursuing prosperity. It's about pursuing purpose. **SARAH ROBBINS**

In network marketing, there are a lot of ranks and titles; there are some great examples of leadership and some not-so-great examples. Notice the kind of leader and example you want to be. Be careful not to confuse ranks with leadership; do not confuse titles or the size of your checks with who you are. You are who God says you are. Rest in that. Step into that. Ranks are stepping stones, markers along the way. They're clever designs by companies to help you run the next lap. Enjoy them and enjoy helping others achieve them, but do not base your definition of yourself or others by title or size of cheque.

REFLECTION: Have I been treating rank like a milestone or letting it define me? Do I treat everyone the same or do I treat people based on rank?

DIVINE STEP FOR SUCCESS

Ask the Holy Spirit to give you understanding and discernment around leadership, your team, and your definition of self. Lift up your team to God—those who have gone dormant, those who are currently building, and your future team. Is there someone who you could give a leadership task to today? Is there a way that you could offer your leadership to your upline?

RAISING *Hallelujah*

PATH

- [ ] **PRAY**
- [ ] **THANKS**
- [ ] **AFFIRMATIONS**
- [ ] **HALLELUJAH**

FIRES

- [ ] **FOLLOW UP**
- [ ] **INVITE**
- [ ] **RECONNECT**
- [ ] **EXPAND**
- [ ] **SOCIAL POSTS**

TWO
Sticks

WHAT GOD SAYS ABOUT YOU . . .

YOU ARE BOLD AS A LION *PROVERBS 28:1 AMP*

I am _____

YOU ARE DO ALL THINGS THROUGH HIM
PHILIPPIANS 4:13 NIV

I am _____

YOU ARE CREATED FOR GOOD WORKS
EPHESIANS 2:10 ESV

I am _____

YOU ARE A CHILD OF GOD *ISAIAH 64:8 NIV*

I am _____

YOU ARE CALLED INTO THE LIGHT
1 PETER 2:9 NIV

I am _____

YOU ARE DECLARED HOLY
1 CORINTHIANS 6:11 AMP

I am _____

YOU ARE ENRICHED IN ALL KNOWLEDGE
1 CORINTHIANS 1:5 ESV

I am _____

YOU ARE A FELLOW CITIZEN *EPHESIANS 2:19
NIV*

I am _____

YOU ARE FREE *JOHN 8:36 ESV*

I am _____

YOU ARE FREE FROM ALL SIN
ROMANS 6:22 AMP

I am _____

God has given you two sticks.

God has called you to build a business that is going to take two sticks and some consistency. I sometimes imagine back to the time when the only way to have a fire was lightning and how if you had fire you had to keep it going for the survival of your village. So you had to keep that fire burning no matter what—never let it go out.

Then a rumor. A rumor you can get a fire started by rubbing two sticks together. I wonder what happened? Who jumped up and looked for two sticks? Who waited to see how others would try? Who bad-mouthed the idea and mocked those who believed? Sound familiar? Have you ever had someone mock you for your belief in your opportunity? Or your belief in a higher power?

Rubbing two sticks together took faith in the beginning, and so does building your business. It will be the consistency of that action and faith that creates the spark.

Sometimes we are called to do something that feels too big, so instead, we procrastinate or run the other way. Jonah was like that. God asked him to do something big.

God asked Jonah to "Go to Ninevah and preach to the people."

(Ninevah was in a bad way with tons of sinning, excessive wickedness, and violent citizens)

Jonah flat out thought, "ME? NO WAY." He ran completely the other way. He jumped on a ship to take him in the opposite direction. When there was a mighty storm and the sailors found out he was running from God and they could not get back to land, they did the only thing they thought might appease God and threw Jonah overboard.

As the story goes, God appointed a great fish to swallow Jonah. Alone and afraid in the belly of the whale, Jonah prayed; surrounded by bile and darkness, he remembered God.

After three days of blackness, God ordered the fish to throw up Jonah, bile and all, onto the beach, and then as Jonah stood, God commanded him again.

"Go to Ninevah and preach to the people . . ."

This is the part that gets me. How many times does one avoid a calling and experience storms, bile, and dark days only to come right back around to the calling? How much easier could it have been for Jonah had he listened the first time? The calling on Jonah did not change. He just got in his own way, made it harder, and ran from what he needed to do.

After that second command, he chose to obey and went. Jonah did the hard stuff, preached, showed up day after day obeying God. What is God calling you to do? Are you headed in the right direction daily? Or are you running the other way? Procrastinating? Paralyzed? Scared? Tired? Lean in and follow the call; there tends to be less bile and darkness the more direct way.

Yet you, Lord, are our Father. We are the clay, you are the potter;
we are all the work of your hand.
ISAIAH 64:8 NIV

DATE _____

Forget about what's happened; don't keep going over old history. Be alert, be present. I'm about to do something brand-new. It's bursting out! Don't you see it? There it is! I'm making a road through the desert, rivers in the badlands. **ISAIAH 43:18-19 MSG**

You first expected the results you currently have in your life. Change your expectations, and you will change your life. **RAY HIGDON**

Forget old history. Don't keep going over what has gone wrong in the past. Maybe this is not your first try, your first company; maybe you had a large team, but now it's smaller; maybe you have never had a team. Perhaps there have been moments in the past that still define how you show up today. Today is a new day. Today is the day to plant new seeds and create new expectations and new results.

REFLECTION: Have I been beating myself up for what I should have done instead of looking toward what could be done today? Is there an old trauma, memory, or experience that is still defining me? If I could rewrite that definition, what would it be?

DIVINE STEP FOR SUCCESS

Starting today, remove "should" from your vocabulary and replace it with "could."
Should is filled with guilt and regret. Could is filled with possibility.
What could God help you with today?

For example: "I should prospect today" instead of "I could prospect today."
Which sentence is more motivating?

R A I S I N G *Hallelujah*

PATH

- [ ] **PRAY**
- [ ] **THANKS**
- [ ] **AFFIRMATIONS**
- [ ] **HALLELUJAH**

FIRES

- [ ] **FOLLOW UP**
- [ ] **INVITE**
- [ ] **RECONNECT**
- [ ] **EXPAND**
- [ ] **SOCIAL POSTS**

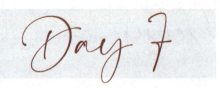

DATE _____

Therefore I tell you, whatever you ask for in prayer, believe that you have received it, and it will be yours. **MARK 11:24 NIV**

I cry out to God Most High, to God who fulfills his purpose for me. **PSALM 57:2 ESV**

The message. Over and over in the Bible is one of hope, faith, and creation. Ask, and you shall receive; what you speak will come to fruition.

REFLECTION: If what you spoke out immediately manifested into reality, would you speak out differently? If you absolutely believed what you spoke out would come to fruition, what would you speak out?

DIVINE STEP FOR SUCCESS

Write out what would be different if you had that dream check coming in. How would you feel? Picture it as if you are remembering it. What would you spend it on? Who would you share it with? Write it out. What is your dream monthly income? How would you show up differently? How would it feel?

DIVINE TIP!

When speaking out financial goals, always add a plus sign to the number. (example: 10,000+ monthly)

RAISING *Hallelujah*

PATH

- [ ] **PRAY**
- [ ] **THANKS**
- [ ] **AFFIRMATIONS**
- [ ] **HALLELUJAH**

FIRES

- [ ] **FOLLOW UP**
- [ ] **INVITE**
- [ ] **RECONNECT**
- [ ] **EXPAND**
- [ ] **SOCIAL POSTS**

DATE _____

Ask, and the gift is yours. Seek, and you'll discover. Knock, and the door will be opened for you. For every persistent one will get what he asks for. Every persistent seeker will discover what he longs for. And everyone who knocks persistently will one day find an open door. **MATTHEW 7:7,8 TPT**

If you fight for your limitations, you might just get to keep them.. **ONA BROWN**

Rubbing two sticks together is action. Persistent action. What are you fighting for? What are you being persistent about . . . what you want or what you don't want? Are you persistently describing yourself as a quick learner? Favored? Growing? We always have more than enough, and I'm full of energy! OR . . . I'm so busy, there isn't enough time, I am messy, I'm terrible at . . . We never have any money, I'm always tired, and my team isn't doing anything, etc.

God has GOT this! He will open doors for you; he will also close doors for you.

REFLECTION: What am I speaking out persistently? When did God close a door that I can look back on now and thank him for? What doors has he opened? What doors are you knocking on?

DIVINE STEP FOR SUCCESS

Moving forward, notice where you speak what you don't want. Picture a stop sign, then replace what you're saying with words that you do want. If you were to open a door and everything you wanted was behind it, what would be there? What would it feel like? Give that glory to God.

RAISING *Hallelujah*

PATH

- [ ] **PRAY**
- [ ] **THANKS**
- [ ] **AFFIRMATIONS**
- [ ] **HALLELUJAH**

FIRES

- [ ] **FOLLOW UP**
- [ ] **INVITE**
- [ ] **RECONNECT**
- [ ] **EXPAND**
- [ ] **SOCIAL POSTS**

DATE _____

It [the Kingdom] is like a mustard seed, which is the smallest of all seeds you plant in the ground. Yet when planted, it grows and becomes the largest of all garden plants, with such big branches that the birds of the air can perch in its shade. **MARK 4:31-32 NIV**

Anything you can imagine you can create. **OPRAH**

Each day as we build our businesses, we plant seeds. Some of the seeds will remain dormant forever or for a term. Our job is to plant intentionally with God. Have faith that the seeds that are meant to grow will grow, trusting there will be a harvest like the bird that begins to sing right before the sun rises in anticipation and faith of a new day.

REFLECTION: Am I planting seeds daily with faith? Take a moment and ask yourself, "Is my energy on the planted or the planting?"

DIVINE STEP FOR SUCCESS

Take a moment and pray for every seed you've ever planted. Today increase your reach outs. Double your normal inviting. How can you push yourself a little so that it is a stretch but not a strain?

DIVINE TIP!

Nurture customers and team with personalized cards and gifts see my favorite Resource (listed in the back of the planner) for this! They personalize, stuff, stamp and deliver for you!

RAISING *Hallelujah*

PATH

- [ ] **PRAY**
- [ ] **THANKS**
- [ ] **AFFIRMATIONS**
- [ ] **HALLELUJAH**

FIRES

- [ ] **FOLLOW UP**
- [ ] **INVITE**
- [ ] **RECONNECT**
- [ ] **EXPAND**
- [ ] **SOCIAL POSTS**

DATE_____

Searching for it [God's counsel] like a prospector panning for gold, like an adventurer on a treasure hunt. **PROVERBS 2:4 MSG**

You can be terrible; as long as you are consistent, you'll make something happen.
JESSICA HIGDON

Imagine a prospector panning for gold, sitting at the edge of the river, knowing gold is in the dirt, staring at the water passing. Not moving the dirt, just staring at it. Hour after hour. Day after day. Leaving the site to find a bigger pan, perhaps moving to a different spot. Researching machines . . . taking courses on how to move the pan, place the pan, sift the dirt . . . but never actually getting their hands wet. Are you in action? Are you moving the dirt? Looking for gold?

REFLECTION: What am I avoiding because I need it to be perfect? What is an area I can show up imperfectly in to grow today? What's something I am not doing because I don't feel ready?

DIVINE STEP FOR SUCCESS

Commit to doing something you are scared of or have been avoiding. Commit to do it with God. Write a letter to God telling him why you are not doing the thing, then thank him and praise him for helping you with completing this task.

RAISING *Hallelujah*

PATH

- [ ] **PRAY**
- [ ] **THANKS**
- [ ] **AFFIRMATIONS**
- [ ] **HALLELUJAH**

FIRES

- [ ] **FOLLOW UP**
- [ ] **INVITE**
- [ ] **RECONNECT**
- [ ] **EXPAND**
- [ ] **SOCIAL POSTS**

THE
Spark

WHAT GOD SAYS ABOUT YOU . . .

YOU ARE FRUITFUL *DEUTERONOMY 7:13 AMP*

I am _____

YOU ARE GIFTED *1 CORINTHIANS 1:7 NIV*

I am _____

YOU ARE GIVEN ALL THINGS
1 CORINTHIANS 1:7 NIV

I am _____

YOU HAVE THE MIND OF CHRIST
ROMANS 8:9 ESV

I am _____

HE IS AT WORK IN YOU
2 CORINTHIANS 4:12 AMP

I am _____

HE IS FOR YOU NOT AGAINST YOU
JOSHUA 1:9 AMP

I am _____

YOU ARE HEALED *ACTS 3:16 AMP*

I am _____

YOU ARE INCREASING IN THE KNOWLEDGE
OF GOD *1 CORINTHIANS 1:5 ESV*

I am _____

YOU ARE INSEPARABLE FROM THE LOVE OF
GOD *1 CORINTHIANS 6:19 AMP*

I am _____

YOU ARE A JOINT HEIR WITH JESUS
GALATIANS 4:7 NIV

I am _____

Faith in the Spark.

The Spark . . . I can imagine it would have taken a lot of faith back in the day. Believing the rumors that two sticks could start a fire.

But that spark.

Oh, when it sparked.

It must have been exciting.

Then you would want to tell the world! It works!

In the beginning of building our businesses, imagining the spark and the growing fire helps us stay on task. Helping our team believe without seeing, showing them how they can build their own fire. Oh, the faith that requires. It is not for everyone.

Faith is something Elijah had in spades. You can find the story in 1 Kings 18:1-40.

Courage is required to build your business, and courage requires faith. When Elijah faced his enemies up on the mountain, he did so with fire in his heart. No one had seen an underdog rise up like this since David and Goliath, a far distant story from years before.

Elijah literally called down the fire from God.

He called down the fire and lit the impossibly wet offering surrounded by a trench of water.

After the fire was lit and the people saw the power of God, the story continued. Elijah believed for rain. After an unbelievable drought, he believed. And the rains came.

Leadership requires faith and courage. Without courage and faith, it is impossible to bring about change, stand for a new future, or put action into a new vision God has put on our hearts.

We read about Elijah calling down the fire from heaven and see his conviction in his purpose from God, his need for God, his faith, his willingness to face circumstances only God's fire would light. His compassion outweighed his difficulties, his desire outweighed his hardship, and his resolve outweighed his hesitancies.

Stand firm in your vision from God; resolve to see it through.

. . . For this reason, since the day we heard about you, we have not stopped praying for you and asking God to fill you with the knowledge of His will in all spiritual wisdom and understanding, so that you may walk in a manner worthy of the Lord and may please Him in every way: bearing fruit in every good work, growing in the knowledge of God, being strengthened with all power according to His glorious might so that you may have full endurance and patience, and joyfully . .

COLOSSIANS 1:9-11 BSB

DATE _____

Look to the Lord and his strength; seek his face always.
1 CHRONICLES 16:11 NIV

Motivation is what gets you started. Habit is what keeps you going. **JIM ROHN**

Sometimes we try to build this business on our own. There are many habits that can help with building a strong business daily: prospecting, following up, posting on social media, expanding our networks, and our daily methods of operation (DMO). Many people lose motivation when they don't see immediate results. Instead of seeking results, seek God first, and include him in every action, large and small. Including him in your daily business-building routine will dissolve blocks and help you see where you need to focus.

REFLECTION: Is it my habit to look to God when I lose my motivation or feel fear around showing up consistently? If not, what is my habit when I face a lack of motivation or feel fear?

DIVINE STEP FOR SUCCESS

Put 5 tiny things you can do when you are resisting showing up the way you want to into the notes app on your phone. For example: wanting to reach out to 20 people a day, but day after day you don't do it? Go to the notes app in your phone and do one or more of the following: Seek God, pray for motivation, visualize yourself in action, set a timer for one minute and prospect, set a timer for one minute and follow up, set a timer for one minute and post, play a motivating playlist (music which makes you feel good!), stand on scripture, etc.

DIVINE TIP!
Write out in your planner one extra thing you would love to get done this week!

RAISING *Hallelujah*

PATH

- ☐ **PRAY**
- ☐ **THANKS**
- ☐ **AFFIRMATIONS**
- ☐ **HALLELUJAH**

FIRES

- ☐ **FOLLOW UP**
- ☐ **INVITE**
- ☐ **RECONNECT**
- ☐ **EXPAND**
- ☐ **SOCIAL POSTS**

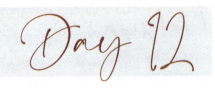

DATE _____

Your word is a lamp to my feet And a light to my path.
PSALM 119:105 AMP

Feed Your faith, starve your doubts. **JOHN C. MAXWELL**

Wherever you are on your journey in network marketing, it can sometimes feel lonely; whether you are a team of one or a team of thousands, there will be times when hope feels far away or courage to do even the little things will feel impossible. In these times, let God's word light your way. When you feel alone in your business or your pursuit of a vision, remember you are never alone; you have the greatest upline of all time in him.

REFLECTION: When I feel lonely or down in my business, where do I automatically turn? (Food, TV, sleep, alcohol, work, negative thoughts, etc.) Does this serve me? Where could I turn instead? (What could I do instead?)

DIVINE STEP FOR SUCCESS

Write down a favorite scripture you can turn to when you feel down. Speak that out then go prospect 3 people and/or follow up with 3 people.
My two favorites are **JEREMIAH 29:11** *and* **JOSHUA 1:9.**

RAISING *Hallelujah*

PATH

- [ ] **PRAY**
- [ ] **THANKS**
- [ ] **AFFIRMATIONS**
- [ ] **HALLELUJAH**

FIRES

- [ ] **FOLLOW UP**
- [ ] **INVITE**
- [ ] **RECONNECT**
- [ ] **EXPAND**
- [ ] **SOCIAL POSTS**

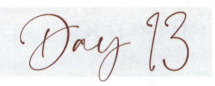

DATE _____

Farmers who wait for perfect weather never plant. If they watch every cloud, they never harvest. **ECCLESIASTES 11:4 NLT**

Perfectionism, whether you like it or not, is a form of procrastination. **RAY HIGDON**

Procrastination . . . Often confused with laziness (procrastinating isn't lazy; it's actively avoiding).

You are not alone if you procrastinate; there are millions of people avoiding the things they don't want to do (but they actually WANT to do . . . crazy, right?). Procrastination is often a masked act of self-protection . . . or rather the two most common reasons for procrastination—fear of success and fear of failure. The fear is the "masked part." These two reasons are usually deeply rooted from when we were kids. Maybe we tried really hard at something and failed, and it hurt so bad. We made it mean, "If I don't try, then I won't cry."

Or maybe the opposite happened. Maybe somewhere along the way, success hurt . . . maybe you shined a bit too bright for someone else's comfort, or maybe someone else felt bad when you shone, which made you uncomfortable.

REFLECTION: Are you procrastinating about your business? Write out what you are avoiding. Ask yourself, "If I played big in this area, how would my life be different? If I keep playing small in this area, who will lose?"

DIVINE STEP FOR SUCCESS

Take a moment and notice what you feel when you are procrastinating about your business. Notice where that feeling is in your body. Imagine that feeling as an object. What color is it? What shape and how much does it weigh? Imagine giving it to God. Do this each time you notice the desire to "not do the work." Don't judge. Be curious, allow, and release. Then step into action, even if only briefly to feel what action feels like instead of procrastination.

RAISING *Hallelujah*

PATH

- [ ] **PRAY**
- [ ] **THANKS**
- [ ] **AFFIRMATIONS**
- [ ] **HALLELUJAH**

FIRES

- [ ] **FOLLOW UP**
- [ ] **INVITE**
- [ ] **RECONNECT**
- [ ] **EXPAND**
- [ ] **SOCIAL POSTS**

DATE _____

So don't sit around on your hands! No more dragging your feet! Clear the path for long-distance runners so no one will trip and fall, so no one will step in a hole and sprain an ankle. Help each other out. And run for it! **HEBREWS 12:12-13 MSG**

It's not about finding great people. It's about becoming a great person. **MARK YARNELL**

Perhaps you have forgotten why you are running; perhaps you are still preparing to run, lacing up your shoes, stretching, watching YouTube videos on how to run. Maybe something happened along the way, such as a sprain, a loss, a hurt, an unexpected turn. It's okay. The amazing thing about this life, this race, this business is that each day is a new day.

REFLECTION: If today were dreamy and you showed up exactly as you wanted to, what would that look like (be specific)? How would it feel?

DIVINE STEP FOR SUCCESS

Brain dump (write out all your thoughts of what you would like to get done) anything that has been weighing on you to complete (for example, clearing a closet, organizing your office, paying a bill, submitting your taxes, reaching out to a friend, forgiving someone). Then schedule one task a week for the next four weeks.

DIVINE TIP!

Keep your planner open and somewhere you can see it Choose colors to highlight important meetings! See my favorite planner in the resource section!

RAISING *Hallelujah*

PATH

- ☐ **P**RAY
- ☐ **T**HANKS
- ☐ **A**FFIRMATIONS
- ☐ **H**ALLELUJAH

FIRES

- ☐ **F**OLLOW UP
- ☐ **I**NVITE
- ☐ **R**ECONNECT
- ☐ **E**XPAND
- ☐ **S**OCIAL POSTS

DATE _____

The person who lives in right relationship with God does it by embracing what God arranges for him. Doing things for God is the opposite of entering into what God does for you . . . "The person who believes God, is set right by God—and that's the real life."
GALATIANS 3:11-12 MSG

Network marketing gives you the opportunity to face your fears, deal with them, overcome them, and bring out the winner that you have living inside of you.
ROBERT KIYOSAKI

Doing things a certain way because someone is looking or because God is looking is living life by performance. We can get tangled up in pretenses pretty quickly in the business of network marketing, where leaders posture and "manage." The world of social media doesn't make this easier. Leading by example and being vulnerable and authentic builds strength, faith, character, and team. Do things for God with God. It all begins with acceptance—acceptance of self and others and the reality of how we are truly showing up.

REFLECTION: Is there any part of my business in which I am telling others to do something, but I am not showing up in that area?

DIVINE STEP FOR SUCCESS

Are you using a timer to do your activities? If not, try it today. Make sure you are setting the timer for each activity to see how long each action in your PATH FIRES takes. For longer tasks, break into increments no longer than 15 mins each. Thirteen to fifteen minutes has been shown to be an ideal amount of time for an adult to focus before they get distracted. Example: Set a timer and invite people to check out your product. How many people did you reach out to in 15 minutes?

RAISING *Hallelujah*

PATH
- ☐ **PRAY**
- ☐ **AFFIRMATIONS**
- ☐ **THANKS**
- ☐ **HALLELUJAH**

FIRES
- ☐ **FOLLOW UP**
- ☐ **INVITE**
- ☐ **RECONNECT**
- ☐ **EXPAND**
- ☐ **SOCIAL POSTS**

FUEL FOR THE *Fire*

WHAT GOD SAYS ABOUT YOU . . .

THE KINGDOM OF GOD IS WITHIN YOU
1 CORINTHIANS 6:19 AMP

I am _____

YOU ARE JUSTIFIED *GALATIANS 2:16 ESV*

I am _____

YOU ARE KNOWN BY HIM *GALATIANS 4:9 ESV*

I am _____

YOU ARE THE LIGHT OF THE WORLD
MATTHEW 5:14 NIV

I am _____

YOU ARE A LIVING STONE *1 PETER 2:5 NIV*

I am _____

YOU ARE MADE IN HIS IMAGE *1 JOHN 3:2 AMP*

I am _____

YOU ARE GOD'S MASTERPIECE
EPHESIANS 2:10 NLT

I am _____

YOU ARE MORE THAN A CONQUEROR
ROMANS 8:37 AMP

I am _____

YOU ARE GOD'S CREATION *ISAIAH 64:8 NIV*

I am _____

YOU ARE A SOUND MIND
2 CORINTHIANS 5:13 NIV

I am _____

Fueling the Fire.

David spent a lot of time getting good at collecting fuel for the fire long before he ever beat Goliath or became king.

Day after day, he practiced. He practiced the harp (which ended up being his ticket to hang with the king). He practiced throwing stones to kill anything that tried to attack his sheep. He practiced for hours and hours and hours.

Les Brown once said, "It's better to be prepared for an opportunity and not have one than to have an opportunity and not be prepared." And I can't think of a more perfect quote.

Can you imagine what it was like to be David before he beat Goliath? He was the youngest son. He stayed behind with the sheep while his older, cooler brothers went off to war.

While he tended the sheep, he did a couple of things that prepared him for the opportunity God was about to lay at his feet.

When the prophet Samuel came to Jesse (David's father) to anoint one of his sons as king, Jesse paraded all of his sons except for David in front of the prophet. Samuel, listening to God, rejected each one as the future king and asked Jesse, "Do you have no other sons?" Jesse then called for David, the youngest, and Samuel anointed David, who would be one day the king.

Here's the thing about this part in the story:

David then goes back to his sheep.

He goes back to practicing his harp and slinging stones to prepare for any kind of attack. David went back to being the best sheepherder he could be.

I don't know about you, but I might have been freaking out a little. ME? KING? HOW? What should I do now? How will it happen? It's not possible. I'm the youngest. I'm the runt. I'm no one. Who am I to be king . . . seriously? I just go back to watching the sheep?

David was anointed to be king, yet he kept showing up and doing the work in front of him, the work he knew. He was preparing, not stressing or posturing about his new anointing.

He kept practicing throwing stones, so he would be prepared should a lion show up to take one of his sheep—he could kill it with a well-aimed blow (which ended up being his secret weapon against Goliath). He kept collecting fuel and getting really good at building the fire in front of him. All of these seemingly small, daily tasks led to the eventual and perfectly aligned plan for him to be king.

Perhaps you feel an anointing on your life. Perhaps you are like David before the anointing. What do you know how to do that you can do daily? How can you collect fuel and build your current fire? What could you work on to prepare for the anointing, the call?

God, your God, is with you every step you take.
JOSHUA 1:9 MSG

DATE _____

So, no matter what I say, what I believe, and what I do, I'm bankrupt without love. Love never gives up. Love cares more for others than for self. Love doesn't want what it doesn't have. Love doesn't strut, Doesn't have a swelled head, Doesn't force itself on others, Isn't always "me first," Doesn't fly off the handle, Doesn't keep score of the sins of others, Doesn't revel when others grovel, Takes pleasure in the flowering of truth, Puts up with anything, Trusts God always, Always looks for the best, Never looks back, But keeps going to the end.
1 CORINTHIANS 13:3-7 MSG

Never forget that 80 percent of your team is happy just to be there. Make them feel good, and they'll stay forever. **RAY HIGDON**

It's likely you have heard of the 80/15/5 rule. Eighty percent of your team won't do a lot, fifteen percent will do a little more, and five percent will do A LOT. One common mistake people make when building a team is to push everyone as if they are in that top 5 percent. The problem with that approach is that most people will leave when they feel pushed and under-appreciated. People show up and stay when they feel loved and appreciated and when they feel a sense of belonging. Appreciate and love every team member regardless of their level of desire. An appreciated team has a high "stickiness" factor.

REFLECTION: Am I frustrated with my team or team members for not showing up in a certain way? For not caring the same way I do? How can I shift that energy to empathy, patience? Where can I pour love on my team?

DIVINE STEP FOR SUCCESS

Do an action of appreciation with no expectation of reciprocation. LOVE ON your team. Whether it is throwing an appreciation ZOOM party with prizes and silly recognition titles or reaching out to each team member. Or even a quick post or message in a group thread. Let them know you LOVE them. All love.

RAISING *Hallelujah*

PATH

- [ ] **P**RAY
- [ ] **T**HANKS
- [ ] **A**FFIRMATIONS
- [ ] **H**ALLELUJAH

FIRES

- [ ] **F**OLLOW UP
- [ ] **I**NVITE
- [ ] **R**ECONNECT
- [ ] **E**XPAND
- [ ] **S**OCIAL POSTS

DATE _____

In God's presence I'll dance all I want! **2 SAMUEL 6:22 MSG**

There is a direct connection between what you feel when you do a behavior and the likelihood that you will repeat the behavior in the future. **BJ FOGG**

Celebrating is such a simple way to shift your feelings around any and all activities! This is why it is so powerful each day to Raise Hallelujah and show others how to do so. Embed celebration and praise into all you do. I have taken this so far that I do a little dance and shout out to God when I do the small things like getting the laundry put away or finishing my morning kitchen-cleaning routine, and yes, I raise a hallelujah and smile each time I reach out to a prospect and each time someone wants more info!

REFLECTION: What's something I do daily that I don't totally love that I could celebrate? Shift your energy and attitude around that activity. What is my energy when I reach out to people to see if they are open to my opportunity? How could I shift that energy? Can you do every task, small and large, for God?

DIVINE STEP FOR SUCCESS

Dance in God's presence while doing a task you have never fully embraced. Do the task and immediately celebrate (smile in the mirror and say, "I did it! Great job!"). Do a fist pump and say, "YES!" Enlist your kids/family/team to come up with a celebration action/dance and do it together daily! Learn to celebrate!

RAISING *Hallelujah*

PATH

- ☐ **PRAY**
- ☐ **THANKS**
- ☐ **AFFIRMATIONS**
- ☐ **HALLELUJAH**

FIRES

- ☐ **FOLLOW UP**
- ☐ **INVITE**
- ☐ **RECONNECT**
- ☐ **EXPAND**
- ☐ **SOCIAL POSTS**

DATE _____

. . . but He has said to me, "My grace is sufficient for you [My loving kindness and My mercy are more than enough—always available—regardless of the situation]; for [My] power is being perfected [and is completed and shows itself most effectively] in [your] weakness." Therefore, I will all the more gladly boast in my weaknesses, so that the power of Christ [may completely enfold me and] may dwell in me. **2 CORINTHIANS 12:9 AMP**

The decisions you make today will limit or expand the choices you have in the future. **VANESSA HUNTER**

Good news! Your weaknesses are not an accident; they are opportunities to lean into God and use his power. Lean in! Get excited. This is your opportunity to grow and give the glory to God and feel the Holy Spirit alive in you.

REFLECTION: Where do I feel weak? Where can I ask for help? My consistency? My social media? My prospecting? My conversations with people? My confidence?

DIVINE STEP FOR SUCCESS

Spend a few minutes each day as you fall asleep picturing yourself doing the action you most wish to take/shift. Picture yourself doing it well, thanking and praising God for the help. Imagine yourself giving God the glory to a friend for those accomplished actions . . . ahead of time.

RAISING *Hallelujah*

PATH

- ☐ **PRAY**
- ☐ **THANKS**
- ☐ **AFFIRMATIONS**
- ☐ **HALLELUJAH**

FIRES

- ☐ **FOLLOW UP**
- ☐ **INVITE**
- ☐ **RECONNECT**
- ☐ **EXPAND**
- ☐ **SOCIAL POSTS**

DATE _____

I have it all planned out—plans to take care of you, not abandon you, plans to give you the future you hope for. **JEREMIAH 29:11 MSG**

Every breakthrough is born out of a shift in viewpoint that transforms how a set of circumstances is perceived.
JORDAN ADLER

When I first became a believer, I was excited and saw God in everything I did. One of my friends said I was "on fire for God." This happens when we first get started in our businesses, too. I've heard it called ignorance on fire. It can be hard from this place of excitement and belief to understand why everyone else can't see what we can see. Conversely, you may have lost that "fire" or vision yourself. You can ask God for renewed faith, vision, and empathy for those who cannot "see" what you are immersed in so fully.

REFLECTION: Am I on fire for God? Am I still on fire for my business? Do I have empathy for those who are not in the same place of faith/desire as me?

DIVINE STEP FOR SUCCESS

Get fired up on purpose today! Don't wait! Play some inspirational music, grab an invigorating essential oil, do jumping jacks, get pumped! Take those few moments to step into the "fired up self." What does it feel like to be pumped up, excited, and celebrating action? Choose to step into that action and feeling today.

RAISING *Hallelujah*

PATH

- [ ] **PRAY**
- [ ] **THANKS**
- [ ] **AFFIRMATIONS**
- [ ] **HALLELUJAH**

FIRES

- [ ] **FOLLOW UP**
- [ ] **INVITE**
- [ ] **RECONNECT**
- [ ] **EXPAND**
- [ ] **SOCIAL POSTS**

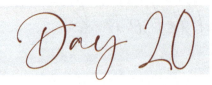

DATE _____

For this reason I remind you to fan into flame the gift of God, which is in you through the laying on of my hands. For God has not given us a spirit of fear, but of power, love, and self-control.
2 TIMOTHY 1:6-7 BSB

We are what we believe we are. **C. S. LEWIS**

Who does God say we are? We are children of the most high God, and God made each and every one of us unique. We are here to bring light with our purpose. What is your brand? Who would God say you are? Who would your 3 closest friends say you are? Who would YOU say you are?

REFLECTION: Am I clear on who I am? What do I love to talk about, learn about, and share? How can I add value to peoples' lives?

DIVINE STEP FOR SUCCESS

Write out 3-5 things you love to share, learn about, and talk about and plan your posts for the next 7 days of social media. How can you add value to other peoples' lives through the interests God has put on your heart?

DIVINE TIP!

Pick one theme for the week and talk about it in a few different ways. Check out my blog on how to plan your social media for 30 days.

RAISING *Hallelujah*

PATH

- ☐ **P**RAY
- ☐ **T**HANKS
- ☐ **A**FFIRMATIONS
- ☐ **H**ALLELUJAH

FIRES

- ☐ **F**OLLOW UP
- ☐ **I**NVITE
- ☐ **R**ECONNECT
- ☐ **E**XPAND
- ☐ **S**OCIAL POSTS

INVITING TO THE *Fire*

WHAT GOD SAYS ABOUT YOU . . .

YOU ARE PREPARED FOR GOOD WORKS
EPHESIANS 2:10 NIV

I am _____

YOU ARE PROTECTED   **ISAIAH 54:17 AMP**

I am _____

YOU ARE PURIFIED   **JOHN 15:13 NLT**

I am _____

YOU ARE REDEEMED   **GALATIANS 3:13 NIV**

I am _____

YOU ARE A ROYAL PRIESTHOOD
1 PETER 2:9 BSB

I am _____

YOU ARE SANCTIFIED   **ACTS 20:32 AMP**

I am _____

YOU ARE THE SALT OF THE EARTH
MATTHEW 5:13 NIV

I am _____

YOU ARE SAVED   **1 CORINTHIANS 15:2 NLT**

I am _____

YOU ARE SEATED WITH HIM IN HEAVENLY
PLACES   **EPHESIANS 2:6 NLT**

I am _____

YOU ARE THE SHEEP OF HIS PASTURE
PSALM 95:7 NIV

I am _____

Moses had Stage Fright . . .

Inviting people to build a business with us can be a little daunting, even knowing that we have a gift, an opportunity that could change lives.

One of my favorite examples of God equipping the unequipped is Moses.

God essentially asked Moses to invite his people to join him, to leave behind their shackles and follow God with him.

He was called to lead his people out of Egypt, and he was scared.

Many of us feel called to build our businesses for many different reasons, and though we know God has put that call on our heart for our own reasons—a stay-at-home job to get more quality time with the kids, to change lives with our product or service, or to add more fun, income, or community into our lives and the lives of others—it can also feel confusing. Maybe you know why; maybe you don't. I knew I wanted to change lives. I had no idea that I would not only change lives, but my own life would also be transformed. I couldn't imagine that network marketing would be the vehicle God would use to help me step into writing, speaking, leadership, coaching, training, and health while healing my anxiety and connecting me with many mentors and positive people. Maybe there is some part of you holding back because you are afraid—afraid to be pushy, afraid to fail, afraid to shine, afraid to lead, afraid to follow, afraid to trust . . . Afraid to ask others to believe with you.

When God asked Moses to go and rescue his people from Egypt, Moses basically responded by saying, "Get someone else to do it!" He was scared. He essentially says, "Don't choose ME. I am not equipped."

God does not call the equipped . . . he equips the called.

How God responded to Moses was so beautiful.

He was patient. He responded, "I will be there with you. I will help you." When Moses continued to come up with reasons why he was the wrong guy for the job, God (I always imagine him slightly exasperated but gentle here) allowed Moses to bring his friend.

Your business will have its ups and downs, and there will be many times when you will be required to do what you do not feel equipped to do. Trust that God is with you. He has laid this calling on your heart. He has answered your prayers. He will be there with you for the entire journey.

Lean on him as your foundation. Invite others to join you in building your fire. Trust that you will receive guidance and help from God; he will answer your prayers and connect you with the right people.

Then the LORD passed by in front of him, and proclaimed, "The LORD, the LORD God, compassionate and gracious, slow to anger, and abounding in lovingkindness and truth (faithfulness) . . .

EXODUS 34:6 AMP

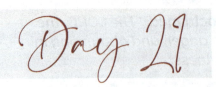

DATE _____

So we're not giving up. How could we! Even though on the outside it often looks like things are falling apart on us, on the inside, where God is making new life, not a day goes by without his unfolding grace. These hard times are small potatoes compared to the coming good times, the lavish celebration prepared for us. There's far more here than meets the eye. The things we see now are here today, gone tomorrow. But the things we can't see now will last forever.
2 CORINTHIANS 4 MSG

...you deal with whatever hard things come up when the time comes. **MATTHEW 6:34 MSG**

In the days that come, there will be days of ease and days of hardship. When things are falling apart around us, we can trust there is a plan, and God is taking care of things on the inside. So if you have an event and no one shows, your team has gone quiet, or someone is offended by your request, keep doing your best and use each hardship as an opportunity to lean on God.

REFLECTION: Often, we have a story of our lives and we look around to collect evidence to make that story real. Take a moment to be grateful for hard times and reflect on what you are grateful for. Collect some new evidence.

DIVINE STEP FOR SUCCESS

Spend time today with God. If he was with you (which he is) like he was with Moses, how would you walk differently. Today wake, walk, drive, pray, and shop as if he is walking with you right now.

RAISING *Hallelujah*

PATH

- [ ] **PRAY**
- [ ] **THANKS**
- [ ] **AFFIRMATIONS**
- [ ] **HALLELUJAH**

FIRES

- [ ] **FOLLOW UP**
- [ ] **INVITE**
- [ ] **RECONNECT**
- [ ] **EXPAND**
- [ ] **SOCIAL POSTS**

DATE _____

If people can't see what God is doing, they stumble all over themselves; But when they attend to what he reveals they are most blessed.
PROVERBS 29:18 MSG

God provides the wind but man must raise the sails.
ST. AUGUSTINE

Trust that God is bringing the right people to your business at the right time. Some will stay a while; some will stay longer. Some will need your tribe, some will run, and some will walk. Some will blossom into leaders and impact thousands of lives. Raise the sails and let God provide the wind. Have a culture that pours love on all of your team. A culture based on love regardless of results will always have a higher "stickiness" versus one based on people's results.

REFLECTION: Do I pour love on my team? How can I encourage a culture of support and encouragement regardless of the level of their desire?

DIVINE STEP FOR SUCCESS

Do a fun post or activity with your team, no matter how big or how small your group is. Share a family moment, a favorite color, a funny face. Book a virtual pajama party or theme party where everyone brings a snack and plays a game.

RAISING *Hallelujah*

PATH

- [ ] **PRAY**
- [ ] **THANKS**
- [ ] **AFFIRMATIONS**
- [ ] **HALLELUJAH**

FIRES

- [ ] **FOLLOW UP**
- [ ] **INVITE**
- [ ] **RECONNECT**
- [ ] **EXPAND**
- [ ] **SOCIAL POSTS**

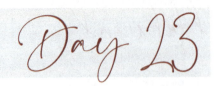

DATE _____

You are the light of the world. A city set on a hill cannot be hidden. Nor do people light a lamp and put it under a basket, but on a stand, and it gives light to all in the house. In the same way, let your light shine before others, so that they may see your good works and give glory to your Father who is in heaven.
MATTHEW 5:14-16 ESV

God didn't make a mistake when he made you. You need to see yourself as God sees you. **JOEL OSTEEN**

God designed you! You are MIRACULOUS! He designed you to be seen, and he has given you unique gifts that no one else has. Where would God say you shine most brightly? How could you shine more in this area? Are you covering your light for fear or dimming it just a bit so as to not be vulnerable? Perhaps shining brightly was frowned upon when you were a child. Maybe when you shone, siblings got in trouble? Perhaps you shone and were made fun of.

REFLECTION: Who in your life shines in an area you would like to shine in as well (think mentors, friends, leaders, uplines)? How do they show up? Could you show up like this?

DIVINE STEP FOR SUCCESS

Identify a mentor you could reach out to or watch more of their trainings. Spend more time around people who you aspire to be more like the person you want to be.

DIVINE TIP!

Find other network marketers from your company or other companies to run with. check out the resource section for my favorite online community to run with.

RAISING *Hallelujah*

PATH

- ☐ **PRAY**
- ☐ **THANKS**
- ☐ **AFFIRMATIONS**
- ☐ **HALLELUJAH**

FIRES

- ☐ **FOLLOW UP**
- ☐ **INVITE**
- ☐ **RECONNECT**
- ☐ **EXPAND**
- ☐ **SOCIAL POSTS**

DATE_____

For God will never give you the spirit of fear, but the Holy Spirit who gives you mighty power, love and self-control.
2 TIMOTHY 1:7 TPT

We have to deal with fear because it is possible that it will make us miss the best parts of life. **JENNIE ALLEN**

Someone once told me that the enemy was like a fly in the eyes of Jesus. That he could easily flick him away. This image is helpful when I feel under attack or need courage. Prayer for protection instantly relieves some discomfort. Our God is an awesome God.

REFLECTION: Where has God given you strength to overcome something that felt impossible?

DIVINE STEP FOR SUCCESS

Do something that scares you today. Reach out to someone on your check-in list, do a Facebook live, share a vulnerable before and after post. Or perhaps call someone and forgive them, or ask for forgiveness from someone.

RAISING *Hallelujah*

PATH

- ☐ **P**RAY
- ☐ **T**HANKS
- ☐ **A**FFIRMATIONS
- ☐ **H**ALLELUJAH

FIRES

- ☐ **F**OLLOW UP
- ☐ **I**NVITE
- ☐ **R**ECONNECT
- ☐ **E**XPAND
- ☐ **S**OCIAL POSTS

DATE _____

In the same way the Spirit [comes to us and] helps us in our weakness. We do not know what prayer to offer or how to offer it as we should, but the Spirit Himself [knows our need and at the right time] intercedes on our behalf with sighs and groanings too deep for words. And He who searches the hearts knows what the mind of the Spirit is, because the Spirit intercedes [before God] on behalf of God's people in accordance with God's will. And we know [with great confidence] that God [who is deeply concerned about us] causes all things to work together [as a plan] for good for those who love God, to those who are called according to His plan and purpose.
ROMANS 8:26-28 AMP

Believe in everyone, count on no one. **STEVE SCHULZ**

You have been called to a purpose, and you have help. Counting on people can be tricky, but counting on God is unfailing. Believe in people and ask for God's help in what to pray for; perhaps you are looking in the wrong direction, praying in a misguided direction, or looking to people instead of God.

REFLECTION: Is there something specific I have been praying for that I could ask for guidance around what I'm praying?

DIVINE STEP FOR SUCCESS

Take a moment and ask the Holy Spirit to intercede for you today in all matters seen and unseen.

RAISING *Hallelujah*

PATH

- ☐ **PRAY**
- ☐ **THANKS**
- ☐ **AFFIRMATIONS**
- ☐ **HALLELUJAH**

FIRES

- ☐ **FOLLOW UP**
- ☐ **INVITE**
- ☐ **RECONNECT**
- ☐ **EXPAND**
- ☐ **SOCIAL POSTS**

MANNING THE
Fire

Firekeeper

WHAT GOD SAYS ABOUT YOU . . .

YOU ARE A SHINING STAR
PHILIPPIANS 2:15 NIV

I am _____

YOU ARE A CHILD OF GOD   **JOHN 1:12-14 BSB**

I am _____

YOU ARE A CHILD OF LIGHT
PHILIPPIANS 2:15 ESV

I am _____

YOU ARE STRENGTHENED BY HIM
PHILIPPIANS 4:13 AMP

I am _____

YOU ARE THE TEMPLE OF GOD
1 CORINTHIANS 6:19 AMP

I am _____

YOU ARE THE TEMPLE OF THE HOLY SPIRIT
1 CORINTHIANS 6:19 AMP

I am _____

YOU ARE TRANSFORMED   **2 CORINTHIANS 3:18**

I am _____

YOU ARE VALUABLE   **MATTHEW 10:31 AMP**

I am _____

YOU ARE GOD'S WORKMANSHIP
EPHESIANS 2:10 BSB

I am _____

YOU ARE WORTHY OF THE LORD
COLOSSIANS 1:10-11 NLT

I am _____

Manning the Fire.

You may have heard the saying, "*Comparison is the thief of joy,*" and this is very important to address in the world of network marketing—worrying about what others are doing, their success and failures, their ranks and paychecks.

There is also the "what others think" phenomenon when we become paralyzed by judgment of others. Will you let what God thinks about you determine your destiny or will you let others throw a wet blanket on your fire?

Manning your fire means guarding your thoughts, praising God for the open and closed doors, celebrating wins, keeping eyes on GOD, and surrounding yourself with people who lead by positive and loving example.

Some people will have their eyes open but just won't see a thing. That's okay . . . Love them where they are but continue to seek God and his instructions for you. Like that famous moment in which Peter is receiving his instructions from Jesus, and he refers to another disciple whom Jesus loved and asks, "What about him?" Jesus responds "What is it to you? As for you, you follow me."

In Luke 8, Jesus shares **The Story of the Seeds:** As they went from town to town, many people joined in and traveled along. He addressed them, using this story: "A farmer went out to sow his seed. Some of it fell on the road; it was tramped down, and the birds ate it. Other seed fell in the gravel; it sprouted but withered because it didn't have good roots. Other seed fell in the weeds; the weeds grew with it and strangled it. Other seed fell in rich earth and produced a bumper crop.

Are you listening to this? Really listening?"

His disciples asked, "Why did you tell this story?"

He said, "You've been given insight into God's kingdom—you know how it works. There are others who need stories. But even with stories, some of them aren't going to get it: Their eyes are open but don't see a thing; their ears are open but don't hear a thing.

"This story is about some of those people. The seed is the Word of God. The seeds on the road are those who hear the Word, but no sooner do they hear it than the Devil snatches it from them, so they won't believe and be saved. The seeds in the gravel are those who hear with enthusiasm, but the enthusiasm doesn't go very deep. It's only another fad, and the moment there's trouble, it's gone. And the seed that fell in the weeds—well, these are the ones who hear, but then the seed is crowded out, and nothing comes of it as they go about their lives worrying about tomorrow, making money, and having fun. But the seed in the good earth—these are the good-hearts who seize the Word and hold on no matter what, sticking with it until there's a harvest."

Some people will not be in a place to hear your message. Man your Fire. There may be wet blankets. Man your Fire. Some people may mock you. Man your Fire. Some may build faster than you. Man your Fire. Focus on YOUR Fire, YOUR God-given mission, HIS Word.

So that the proven character of your faith—more precious than gold, which perishes even though refined by fire—may result in praise, glory, and honor at the revelation of
Jesus Christ..
1 PETER 1:7 BSB

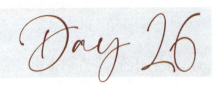

DATE _____

But he's already made it plain how to live, what to do, what God is looking for in men and women. It's quite simple: Do what is fair and just to your neighbor, be compassionate and loyal in your love, and don't take yourself too seriously—take God seriously.
MICAH 6:8 MSG

It's not about how much you do, but how much love you put into what you do that counts. **MOTHER TERESA**

My mother-in-law asked me what she would like me to pray for the other day. She asked, "Your health? Your clients? Your business?" I responded, "Can I ask for wisdom? Oh, and can I ask you to pray for me that I have more energy to show up for God? Oh, oh, oh, can you please pray for me to hear Him better? His calling on my life? Then the energy to show up and do all the "things" he's calling me to do?" She responded, "Of course. God grants us wisdom when we ask for it. I will pray for you." The next day she sent me the above verse that God showed her as she prayed for me. It was so powerful in its simplicity.

I love the perspective of this. And once again, we arrive back at seek God first.

REFLECTION: Where is one area where you feel God may be calling you and it's possible you might be taking yourself too seriously? When you take yourself out of the equation? What does God ask us to do? Be just. Love each other. Serve. Where can you do this with your calling right now? Are you standing in your own way?

DIVINE STEP FOR SUCCESS

*Who could you reach out to today and ask if they need specific prayer?
Is there a team member who comes to mind? Family? A friend?
Pray for someone today.*

RAISING *Hallelujah*

PATH

- [ ] **PRAY**
- [ ] **THANKS**
- [ ] **AFFIRMATIONS**
- [ ] **HALLELUJAH**

FIRES

- [ ] **FOLLOW UP**
- [ ] **INVITE**
- [ ] **RECONNECT**
- [ ] **EXPAND**
- [ ] **SOCIAL POSTS**

DATE _____

Do not judge, or you will be judged. For with the same judgment you pronounce, you will be judged; and with the measure you use, it will be measured to you. **MATTHEW 7:1-2 BSB**

Someone else's opinion of you is none of your business.
RACHEL HOLLIS

Any time you are feeling triggered or judge-y about another's actions, take a moment and reflect upon what might need healing in your own life. "In everything, then, do to others as you would have them do to you . . ." Matthew 7:12 BSB. When you have an emotional reaction to someone else, as quickly as you can, look in the mirror. It is an opportunity to heal.

REFLECTION: Where am I annoyed . . . what's bugging me? Is there something I could heal, forgive, or release in myself?

DIVINE STEP FOR SUCCESS

Reach out today to anyone who has been rubbing you the wrong way and tell them what you appreciate about them. Forgive yourself, too, if that's where the healing needs to start.

DIVINE TIP!

The book BIG LEAP by Gay Henricks is a great book on uncovering limiting beliefs that may be holding you back from shining fully.

RAISING *Hallelujah*

PATH

- ☐ **PRAY**
- ☐ **THANKS**
- ☐ **AFFIRMATIONS**
- ☐ **HALLELUJAH**

FIRES

- ☐ **FOLLOW UP**
- ☐ **INVITE**
- ☐ **RECONNECT**
- ☐ **EXPAND**
- ☐ **SOCIAL POSTS**

DATE _____

"How can I help you?" asked Elisha. "Tell me, what do you have in the house?" She answered, "Your servant has nothing in the house but a jar of oil." "Go," said Elisha, "borrow jars, even empty ones, from all your neighbors. Do not gather just a few . . . they [her sons] kept bringing jars to her, and she kept pouring. When all the jars were full, she said to her son, "Bring me another." But he replied, "There are no more jars." Then the oil stopped flowing. **2 KINGS 4:2-6 BSB**

Study God and his strength, seek his presence day and night; Remember all the wonders He performed.
1 CHRONICLES 16:11 MSG

What do you have that you can be grateful for right now? In the modern-day mishmash of manifesting and creating a dream life, there can be confusion around what is biblical and what ehhh . . . isn't. Focusing on what you have and what you are grateful for is something everyone can agree on. Gratitude leads to multiplication on so many levels. Elisha asked the widow . . . what do you have? They worked on that from there. She collected many pots, even though it made no "realistic" sense . . . had she collected fewer pots, she would have had less oil and more pots she would have had more.

REFLECTION: Are you collecting more pots or fewer? Have you identified your oil? What do you have right now you can be grateful for and multiply?

DIVINE STEP FOR SUCCESS

Post/share a result today. Not a post about your product/service but a post about a result of your product/service. What result can you be grateful for? Create some curiosity.

RAISING *Hallelujah*

PATH

- [ ] **PRAY**
- [ ] **THANKS**
- [ ] **AFFIRMATIONS**
- [ ] **HALLELUJAH**

FIRES

- [ ] **FOLLOW UP**
- [ ] **INVITE**
- [ ] **RECONNECT**
- [ ] **EXPAND**
- [ ] **SOCIAL POSTS**

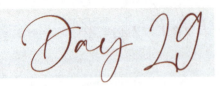

DATE _____

Now to him who is able to do far more abundantly than all that we ask or think, according to the power at work within us.
EPHESIANS 3:20 ESV

You'll never change the world if you are worried about being liked.
RAY HIGDON

Instead of focusing on what others think, good OR bad, focus on what God says. Not only did he give us the Word to focus on, but he also gave us the Holy Spirit, a power at work WITHIN US. Go out there and serve! Change the world with your product, change a family's stars with your opportunity, change someone's life today with finances you earned from your company, or set a goal to do so. You have the power.

REFLECTION: Do I truly believe I have the power within me to achieve great things? If I wiped the slate clean, stepped fully into my God-given power, my God-given gifts, what would I do? Who would I help?

DIVINE STEP FOR SUCCESS

Share the opportunity today to earn some extra money; print out your Facebook friends list and go through it. Who haven't you asked? Go through your phone list starting at A. Who can you text?

RAISING *Hallelujah*

PATH

- ☐ **PRAY**
- ☐ **THANKS**
- ☐ **AFFIRMATIONS**
- ☐ **HALLELUJAH**

FIRES

- ☐ **FOLLOW UP**
- ☐ **INVITE**
- ☐ **RECONNECT**
- ☐ **EXPAND**
- ☐ **SOCIAL POSTS**

DATE _____

And we have come to know and believe the love that God has for us. God is love; and whoever abides in love abides in God, and God in him. **1 JOHN 4:16 BSB**

Leadership: parting the seas with your vision so that others may venture out.
RICHARD BLISS BROOKE

The comfort zone is never truly comfortable. I've always said it's like a bed of nails. It's gonna hurt a little to lie there; it's gonna hurt a little to get up and get going. There is nothing COMFORTABLE about the comfort zone. If others are uncomfortable with the fact that you are growing, changing, and shifting, love them for it. You are highlighting what they are not yet ready to do. If possible, when possible, surround yourself with friends who lift you up, cheer for you, and love and hold the space for friends who do not know how to love you like that. God sets an amazing example of loving us and all our broken bits. It is beautiful when we can do the same for others.

REFLECTION: Do I truly believe I have the power within me to achieve great things? If I wiped the slate clean, stepped fully into my God-given power, my God-given gifts, what would I do? Who would I help?

DIVINE STEP FOR SUCCESS

Write down three people who are already achieving the level of success you want to attain in your business, write down the qualities that you like about them. Is there any way you connect with them through training, reaching out, social media etc? Work on surrounding yourself with people who have achieved the goals you are reaching for.

RAISING *Hallelujah*

PATH
- ☐ **PRAY**
- ☐ **THANKS**
- ☐ **AFFIRMATIONS**
- ☐ **HALLELUJAH**

FIRES
- ☐ **FOLLOW UP**
- ☐ **INVITE**
- ☐ **RECONNECT**
- ☐ **EXPAND**
- ☐ **SOCIAL POSTS**

RESOURCES

Network Marketing

Freakishly Effective Social Media for Network Marketing by Ray and Jessica Higdon

Freakishly Effective Leadership for Network Marketing by Ray and Jessica Higdon

Beach Money by Jordan Adler

The Four-Year Career by Richard Bliss Brooke

Yes, Sometimes It Is About the Money by Steve Schulz

The Big Leap by Gay Henricks

Fearless Networking by Todd Falcone

Go PRO by Eric Worre

Go for No by Richard Fenton, Andrea Waltz, Ray Higdon

Time Money Freedom by Ray and Jessica Higdon

Rock Your Network Marketing Business by Sarah Robbins

The Purpose Driven by Life Rick Warren

Made for This by Jennie Allen

Break Out by Joel Osteen

I Declare by Joel Osteen

One Belief Away by Tim Shurr & Joe Vitale

Put your Dream to the Test by John Maxwell

Favorite Planner And Other Tools

www.Higdongroup.com/planner

www.rankmakershop.com

Favorite Online Community For Network Marketing Training And More

RMU - Rankmakers University

www.rankmakers.com

Bibles Used

The Message (Canvas Bible edition) by Eugene Peterson (MSG)

The Message Devotional Bible by Eugene Peterson (MSG)

English Standard Version Study Bible, Crossway (ESV)

The Maxwell Leadership Bible by John Maxwell (NIV)

Battlefield of the Mind Bible Amplified Version, Joyce Meyer (AMP)

The Passion Translation – the New Testament with Psalms, Proverbs and Song of Songs (TPT)

Berean Study Bible (BSB)

Create Personalized Team Gifts, Cards and Appreciation

https://mailboxpower.com/FIREKEEPER

Check out my website at
www.iamfirekeeper.com
for more for links to my favorite resources!

Made in the USA
Las Vegas, NV
17 October 2023

79256922R20063